MW01251742

TEEC It To The Top!
A Friendly Approach to Literacy Success

Written and Developed by: Nathan Karstulovich

**Robert Munsch
Public School**

Printed in the United States of America

First Printing, 2015

ISBN-13: 9781505428506
ISBN-10: 1505428505

Available for purchase through Amazon.com

www.nathankarstulovich.weebly.com

Cover Photography Copyright © 2013 by Jessica Karstulovich
Edited by Fiona Shaw
Printed by Createspace™ an Amazon.com company.

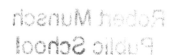

Acknowledgements

Special thanks to Erin, who was the first person to suggest that TEEC was a journey worth pursuing and to Lindsay for believing in the program, working through the early stages and helping to sell its merits to others.

This book is dedicated to my wife Jessica.

TEEC It To The Top!

Table of Contents

Where Did It Start?

In order to fully understand anything worthwhile it is important to understand its history. Although the TEEC system does not have as rich a history as, say, the development of Canada, the reasons behind the TEEC system are important.

First, one must understand that all learners are different. This is important to keep in mind so that a teacher stays focused on the system and does not assume that one piece will cure all literacy ailments. All learners have different personalities, different backgrounds and come to the classroom with different experiences.

When I started teaching, my first assignment was in a grade six class teaching Language and Math. It is an assignment from which many experienced teachers in Ontario tend to shy away due to the pressures of standardized testing. As a first year teacher with a rather large debt upon graduation, I was simply happy to have a job. I had no idea that I was supposed to be stressed about my students' achievement on *the tests*. In fact, shortly after the students completed the assessments, my principal at the time, who was not the principal that hired me, let me know that she "would not assign an inexperienced teacher to teach Language or Math in grade six."

About two months into the school year I realized that my students had the capability of comprehending the texts that they read, however they had a very difficult time talking about it or writing what they knew into paragraphs. After doing some quick research on the provincial assessments and looking at how they were to be scored, I needed to give my students a way to write with fluency and prove that what they were thinking was correct.

I started by talking out the questions that the students were to answer. Together we figured out how to take a question and turn it into a topic to begin a paragraphed answer. Once that became easy, we wrote sentences explaining their knowledge of the texts they were reading. I then spent time brainstorming the best way for my eleven-year-old students to prove that their explanations made sense, which lead me to finding a quote directly from the text being read. Finally, my students were steered to the realization that every completed paragraph needed a conclusion.

Broken down into an anchor chart that even my less academically inclined students could easily remember, I simply wrote in large colourful letters:

Topic
Explanation
Example
Conclusion

And TEEC was born.

Okay, so just a few paragraphs into this book some of you are already saying, "Really? This guy is taking credit for a paragraph format that has been around for many years?"

Absolutely not! I am well aware that TEEC is a paragraph format used in many districts throughout North America. I was first introduced to this paragraph format in high school, although the acronym used was SEEC. The difference was that the S stood for Statement rather than using T for Topic. In fact, if you do a quick Internet search you can find several sites proclaiming the virtues of TEEC and even a few different articles claiming to have created TEEC.

What I hope to provide in this book is a look at the value of using TEEC and some insight into how I have been able to simplify this paragraph structure so that all students can find success. Furthermore, I have been able to assemble a continuum that can be used to develop writing in the TEEC format from grade one through eight.

TEEC is success with simplicity.

What Is TEEC?

TEEC is Topic, Explanation, Example, Conclusion…isn't it? The answer is yes, and no. When I first used what was then a simple paragraph format the answer would have been yes. As I have learned more about teaching, and literacy, and students, the answer has become, no.

The Paragraph

The TEEC paragraph gave students a simple acronym that they could remember easily and helped them develop four simple sentences for a fluent paragraphed answer to a reading comprehension question. Students simply wrote a sentence that confirmed their understanding of what the question was asking, followed it with a second sentence giving their best answer. The big secret to success was to have a quote from the text, in the third sentence, which proved the explanation was reasonable. Then students could add a fourth sentence reiterating their understanding of what they were being asked.

The beauty of the paragraph is that it allows any student to explain and prove their thinking. As long as they have those sentences, who is to say that their interpretation of what is happening in the story is incorrect? Unless you are a grade twelve English teacher who has some sort of psychological connection to the author, you can't possibly know that your explanation is the only true answer. As long as the third sentence quote shows a connection to the explanation it is possible that the student's interpretation is in fact accurate.

However, I couldn't possibly get away with writing a book about four simple sentences. The basis is those four simple sentences but TEEC has grown, for me, from what started out as a four sentence paragraph structure into a much more curriculum aligned, student friendly, literacy system.

The System

Within the broader system I have been able to take the four sentence paragraph structure with which I began and use it to promote the use of reading strategies. In later sections you will see how TEEC helps students to more readily focus on Visualizing, Connecting, Inferring, Determining Importance, Synthesizing and Questioning. The TEEC system helps students to easily see the six traits of good writing – Ideas, Organization, Voice, Word Choice, Fluency, and Conventions. It also allows them to take that knowledge of simple communication and use it to develop larger written works such as essays and reports. Finally, the TEEC system helps students remember to make their point-of-view clear when speaking and debating with others.

Over the past few years I have done several school-based workshops and some Board-wide workshops as well. Most often grade three and grade six teachers would show up hoping for the magic solution to great provincial assessment results. Over the course of a two hour presentation I would hear, several times, "So this is it? Isn't it the same as APE?" or "Isn't this just a Hamburger paragraph?"

On the surface the TEEC system presents a very similar paragraph to the APE (Answer, Proof, Explain) strategy. APE presents a nice memory jogger with the picture of the ape on each poster and APE gives a very similar guideline to writing a paragraph. Both paragraphs look for an answer, an explanation and a proof, however TEEC tends to give students a more concrete expectation to their answers. Students using TEEC know that each letter provides an expectation of one sentence, while APE often needs more than one sentence for each letter of the acronym. In no way do I mean to say that APE is a poor strategy. As a matter of fact, the APE strategy was part of what helped me to understand why students in grade six were struggling with writing paragraph answers to comprehension questions. Many of my students loved the APE strategy. Many of them had been taught the APE strategy in grade four and grade five but most of my students did not actually understand the APE strategy. They were able to give answer to the questions being asked and were often able to explain the reasons behind their thoughts. The students struggled to prove their thinking and connect their proof to their explanation. They also did not know when to stop writing.

This is when TEEC became more than just a paragraph structure and became a literacy system. Using the TEEC system I was able to teach students that the flow of writing is affected by word choice, voice and conventions. By putting the Example (proof) sentence after the Explanation, students realized that these two things must be connected. Also, by sticking to a simple four-sentence format – at first they were not allowed to write any more – students began to understand that more words and more sentences did not always mean better writing

The TEEC system flows through all subjects and all elementary grades. Several students have even come back to me after their grade ten literacy test to tell me that they still use the TEEC system to write their exams. Granted, they usually point out that they have "tweaked it a bit." I think that's great because that means they are now using their own voice in what they write.

The TEEC system begins by teaching students about the paragraph format and then extends into using those four simple sentences to organize thoughts in all subjects and all sorts of written forms. Later in this book you will see examples of how TEEC is used to promote good inquiry techniques and written works.

The Provincial Assessment Question

The other question that I have heard many times from colleagues, from workshop audiences and from Literacy Coaches is, "are you not just teaching to the test?" There seems to be an overriding concern about teaching students to do well on provincial assessments. I have multiple answers to this question. The first is that yes, I am teaching students to write the provincial assessments. Anyone who has administered these assessments knows that if you don't give the students solid strategies to get through it, many students would freeze on the big day. Think about it. If you were given a format that would have helped you show your university professor exactly what she wanted to see on an exam, would that not have been a benefit? In the same respect, a driving instructor who did not give her student an idea of what the driving exam would be like would not be a very good instructor in my mind.

My second answer is also yes, I am teaching to the test. Provincial assessments are meant to analyse whether or not we are preparing our students for higher grades, better learning and ultimately, life outside of the classroom. When I scored the provincial assessments after my first year of teaching it was very evident which students knew how to clearly communicate their thoughts and which students were simply trying to get as many words as possible on the page. By teaching students to write in a fashion that assessment scorers could clearly understand, I am teaching students to write clearly and concisely for an audience that does not know them. That is teaching for the world outside the classroom.

Linking up to my second answer above, my third answer is always no, I am not teaching to the test. The provincial assessments are important but not the main focus of the TEEC system. The TEEC system teaches students to think through what they want to say and then write it in a fashion that is easy to read and understand. That type of writing is useful well beyond any grade three, six, or ten assessment. This type of clear, concise writing is what is currently missing from e-mails, text messages, and many office memos around the country. The clear flow of the TEEC system is exactly the type of writing that will help students comprehend texts, write plausible reports and essays, and be able to tell the world that their voice is important.

The TEEC system is all about clear, concise literacy.

Reading With TEEC

When I talk about reading with TEEC it needs to be understood that the TEEC system is not meant to help students decode and read simple sentences. What the TEEC system does is help students use strategies to comprehend what they are reading. The TEEC system becomes a guide to Visualizing, Questioning, Inferring, Determining Importance and Synthesizing. Once again I will point to the fact that the TEEC system is not a magic bean that will suddenly make everyone richly literate. Teaching the reading comprehension strategies is still a very important task for the classroom teacher. Having the TEEC system guide the students' understanding will make life easier in the long run.

When students are taught to visualize what they are reading, they can begin to see reading as being interesting – just like watching a movie. In one of my early classes my students talked about how great the movie *National Treasure* was. Some of them were unable to understand, however, why the change from standard time to daylight savings time affected where the characters found the special reading glasses. When we acted the scene out and visualized the differences in shadows (along with a quick history lesson on the use of daylight savings time) students were then able to see why the time change was important to the movie.

This movie example helped to show my students the importance of being able to see (or visualize) what is happening. Although those students who saw the movie had a visual given to them, they got the understanding that the visuals that they create help them to understand texts. By working through this activity those students who had not seen the movie had many questions answered and realized that by asking the questions they gained a better understanding of the story and the scene in particular.

The example helped students to understand the importance of all reading strategies and then use those strategies to help build TEEC paragraphs. By using TEEC to answer comprehension questions the other strategies are used and proven easily. For example, let's ask the question: What is the main idea of the story *Beauty and the Beast*?

Given this question I would ask students to consider several things. First of all they would need to visualize what has happened in the story. Hopefully they have learned, through other lessons, to visualize while they are reading. Then they would be expected to question the story. Often I will have students use sticky notes while they read to write down any questions that arise as they are reading.

A standard level grade six answer might look like this:

The main idea of *Beauty and the Beast* is to love people for who they are on the inside. This is the main idea because the story revolves around a monster that turns out to be really kind hearted. In the text it says, "Then it started to say a few kind words, till in the end, Beauty was amazed to discover that she was actually enjoying its conversation. The days passed, and Beauty and the Beast became good friends." The main idea of the story is to love people for who they are on the inside.

If I break down this paragraph I have four sentences.

The Topic sentence restates the question without using the question word and gives a simple answer.

The main idea of *Beauty and the Beast* is to love people for who they are on the inside.

This sentence focuses students on what they are trying to comprehend. It forces them to be able to restate the question themselves and allows their audience to know what they will be writing about without having the question at hand.

The second sentence gives an explanation telling the audience why the writer believes the answer is correct.

This is the main idea because the story revolves around a monster that turns out to be really kind-hearted.

Although these sentences are not terribly creative they get to the point. When teaching a young student to think and communicate through writing it is important to keep it simple until they understand the flow that is needed.

The third sentence shows proof, directly from the text, that the explanation is reasonable.

In the text it says, "Then it started to say a few kind words, till in the end, Beauty was amazed to discover that she was actually enjoying its conversation. The days passed, and Beauty and the Beast became good friends."

This quote becomes a very important point in the paragraph. First of all, it provides proof that the student's explanation makes sense. Secondly, it provides a good teachable moment about the importance of having proof for the things you speak of, and the necessity to use quotation marks when using someone else's words. Finally, by taking a quote directly from the story shows students that their answer must be directly connected to the text they are reading.

The fourth sentence closes the paragraph and ensures that students stay on topic.

The main idea of the story is to love people for who they are on the inside.

It is simple and reiterates the focus on the question at hand.

The other reading comprehension strategies fit in once students have learned to structure the paragraph. After teaching Visualization and Questioning, we begin to talk about Connecting, Inferring, Determining Importance and Synthesizing. All these strategies are what students have actually used to furnish their answer in the first place.

For example, students would have had to determine that loving someone for what is on the inside is an important message in order to deem it to be the main idea. Through discussion we would find out that they can connect to this idea because, maybe, it's a lesson they have been taught at home, or they have heard in church, or they have seen in a movie, and the list goes on. Further, this discussion can lead to an understanding of where we find our connections and how they help us to understand what we read.

No place in the story does it say that one should love someone for who they are in the inside. This is a message that students must infer. This fact again leads to significant discussion about inferences. This simple four-sentence paragraph has led to several significant teachable moments regarding reading comprehension.

Based on what we have just learned about comprehension strategies and the TEEC system you may have noticed that the questions that are asked are very important. If the questions are too simplistic there may not be anything to explain or infer. The classroom teacher must be sure to evaluate the difficulty of the questions and whether or not they pose potential for too little thought or too much confusion.

Questions that make students think may include:
1. Explain 3 characteristics of the main character in your novel.
2. Explain 4 characteristics that show that your novel is either a fictional narrative or a non-fiction piece of writing.
3. What could be added to this book to help you better understand the story or information?
4. What is the main idea of the novel?
5. Use information from the book and your own ideas to explain a personality trait that you believe the author possesses.
6. Compare and contrast the world of your book to the world you live in. Explain which world you would prefer to live in.

As you read through some of the questions you may wonder how the four-sentence TEEC paragraph structure can be used to answer these more in-depth questions. This is why TEEC is a system, not just a structure.

In later sections I will reveal a continuum of templates and structures that are used beginning in grade one and progressing through grade eight.

Why It Works

TEEC works because it's simple! That's right. Keep it simple.

Often teachers, with all good intentions, make things more complex than they need to be. Especially in the upper grades, teachers whom have been teaching the same grade for an extended period of time, have a tendency to think too much about what students will need next year. Grade eight teachers often become focused on high school, or grade six teachers become focused on intermediate grades. As teachers, we need to remember that students go through each grade for a reason. Each year is meant to develop different aspects of the students' abilities. Teachers using the TEEC system need to stay focused on meeting grade level standards. Once those standards have been achieved, only then should students and teachers think about moving beyond grade expectations and shooting for that A+.

The TEEC system works because students are presented with specific success criteria. A grade six student will know that presenting a four-sentence paragraph that includes a topic sentence, explanation, example and conclusion should allow them to achieve the grade level standard-provided that the explanation and example relate to one another.

So far, I have written about all the advantages for grade six students and their reading comprehension. But, how does it help in other grades?

The grade six paragraph was the beginning point and as it turns out it was the perfect point to begin. The TEEC system was then developed upward to grade eight and downward to grade one. TEEC is now a school-wide system that begins in grade one, introducing topics and answers, and flows through to grade eight with a full understanding of how each reading strategy helps a student to better understand what he is reading. The school-wide system is really why the TEEC system works. Students begin learning how to answer questions in grade one and each year a new piece of the paragraph is added or refined. By grade four, students are working with four sentences, refining their understanding of examples into grade six. In grade seven we add connections and students' own ideas and by grade eight students are analyzing how the reading strategies have helped their understanding of what has been read.

The TEEC system works because it is consistent. It works because it is clear. It works because the TEEC system is simple.

Samples and Templates

Get started with these templates.

Samples and Templates

TEEC Paragraph Templates

Remember that the TEEC system is a continuum of expectations beginning in grade one and continuing through grade eight. This section will present each template with an explanation of how and why it is used at each grade level. Also keep in mind, however, that it's never too late to begin using the TEEC system. The first group of students who went through the system started learning about TEEC in grade six. That simply meant that the learning curve was a bit larger but they were able to succeed none-the-less. The biggest piece of new learning – like with many other areas – comes in the primary grades, while the junior grades solidify the use of the paragraph. The templates for intermediate grades help students to solidify their reading comprehension and look within themselves for explanation.

The grade-by-grade explanation is stated beside the corresponding templates throughout this chapter. Some grades provide multiple templates as teachers will find that different templates are needed to cue different students' needs or that some students will be ready for extensions to their learning.

The easiest way to teach students about the paragraph is to break it down into individual sentences first and then develop the paragraph afterward. You will notice short notes alongside each sentence box in the templates that help students remember what to write. The original four-sentence paragraph is broken down like this:

Topic – take the question, eliminate the question word (who, what, where, etc.), and re-write the sentence with an answer.

Explanation – explain why your answer is correct using the work "because" in the sentence.

Example – begin with "In the text it says," and complete the sentence with a quote directly out of the text.

Conclusion – restate the topic sentence.

Paragraph Samples

Along with each template you will see some samples of students' reading comprehension answers done at different time in the year. All selections show the development within each grade. These are meant to show that the students at each grade level can have success using the TEEC system. Like any educational tool used in the classroom there will be different levels of success at different times of the year. Stay positive and you will see that the TEEC system makes answering comprehension questions easier for all students.

Grade One

In grade one the idea is not to have students' writing in paragraphs but simply to introduce them to the TEEC style. Just like learning how to ride a bike, where we start with training wheels and then gradually ride on our own, the TEEC system introduces the paragraph ideas gradually and works toward individual mastery. Grade ones are still learning to write sentences but they can speak well enough to use TEEC. Practising the Topic sentence and moving on to an Explanation sentence orally will help students get used to the format of the paragraph to come. Ideally, a grade one student will be able to write the first two sentences (Topic and Explanation) by the end of the school year. If and when the classroom teacher and the students get around to writing their sentences, there is space on the template for feedback with "Two Stars" and "A Wish" – a feedback response that reveals two good points and one point of improvement for student work.

Student Samples

Question: Why do we come to school?

Grade level answer: We come to school because we need to learn.

Question: Why do we put our names on our papers?

Grade level answer: We put our names on our papers because our teachers need to know that it is ours.

Question: Why do we need to eat healthy snacks?

Grade level answer: We need to eat healthy snacks because we can't be tired in school.

GRADE 1 PARAGRAPH FORMAT
For Answering Reading Response Questions

Topic Sentence (answer the question with part of the question in your answer – delete the W word)	_____ _____ _____ _____
Explanation ("because" sentence that has one or more examples from the text)	_____ _____ _____ _____

2 Stars:

A Wish:

Grade Two

In grade two students should be able to write simple sentences so using the template as a next step, they are introduced to writing in a paragraph. It is important for the grade two students to have access to the template as often as possible. At this level they are expected to be able to write the Topic and Explanation – which they did orally in grade one – and add a Conclusion sentence. In my experience the grade two students tend to enjoy adding the conclusion once they are taught that the conclusion sentence is simply a restate of the topic sentence. "Two Stars" and "A Wish" on the template continue to offer relevant feedback to students.

Student Sample

Question: Why did Lemon need more help than her brothers and sisters (in the book *Lemon The Duck* by Laura Backman)?

Grade level answer: Lemon needed more help than her brothers and sisters. She needed more help because she could not walk or stand. This is why she needed more help than her brothers and sisters.

Question: Was Stella helpful in the book *Goodnight Sam* (by Marie-Louise Gay)?

Grade level answer: Stella was helpful in the book *Goodnight Sam*. She was helping because she was saying "go to bed". She was helpful.

GRADE 2 PARAGRAPH FORMAT
For Answering Reading Response Questions

Topic Sentence (answer the question with part of the question in your answer – delete the W word)	_____ _____ _____ _____
Explanation ("because" sentence that has one or more examples from the text)	_____ _____ _____ _____
Conclusion (restate the Topic sentence)	_____ _____ _____ _____

2 Stars:

A Wish:

Grade Three

By grade three students need to be prepared for provincial assessments. This means that writing in paragraphs is an important skill to have by the end of the school year. Grade three students are expected to be able to complete the full TEEC style paragraph with a small alteration. In grade three, students are taught to link their Explanation and Example by combining the sentences into one. This sentence will allow students to give an answer and then explain that their answer is correct because of something they read in the text.

To extend the learning experience for those students that are deemed ready, the grade three template allows students to add their own connection by stating something that they are reminded of while reading the story.

The grade three template moves from the star and wish idea and instead includes a checklist so that students can peer-edit to ensure all necessary sentences are completed.

Student Sample

Question: Name an important part of a coral reef and explain why it is important.

Grade level answer: Plants are an important part of a coral reef. They are important because in the text it says, "Coral reefs have many places where fish can live and hide". Plants are an important part of a coral reef.

GRADE 3 PARAGRAPH FORMAT
For Answering Reading Response Questions

Topic Sentence (answer the question with part of the question in your answer – delete the W word)	
Explanation ("because" sentence that has one or more examples from the text)	_____ _____ **because in the text it says** " _____ _____ "
Conclusion (restate the Topic sentence)	

Now go back and check…

_____ Does my topic sentence use the question but delete the "W" word?

_____ Does my explanation answer the question and use a sentence from the text?

_____ Do I include what this reminds me of?

_____ Do I conclude by restating the topic sentence?

Grade Four, Five and Six

In the junior grades (four, five and six) it's time for students to solidify their understanding and use of the paragraph structure for answering reading questions. Beginning in grade four students should be introduced to the four TEEC sentences. In grade five students need to be taught to dig deeper into their reading so that the four sentences not only make sense but also reveal the best possible answer to the questions posed. By grade six students should be expected to answer all reading questions that need explanation by using the TEEC paragraph format. This means that even a question that asks students to show two or three different things should be answered in TEEC format. Students can learn to do this by adding Explanation and Example sentences to their answers. In some instances the TEEC paragraph may become the TEEEEEEC paragraph.

The students can extend their understanding by adding specific personal connections to their answers (see the grade 7 template). Again, multiple templates may be needed to introduce the idea of a multi-explanation paragraph and the idea of adding a personal connection. The junior paragraph template includes a checklist at the bottom so that students can double-check their own work to ensure they have included all necessary pieces of the paragraph.

Grade 4 Student Sample

Question: Name an important part of a coral reef and explain why it is important.

Grade level answer: Plants are an important part of a coral reef. They are important because they provide a home, a place to hide and food for fish. In the text it says, "Coral reefs have many places where fish can live and hide". Plants are an important part of a coral reef.

Grade 5 Student Sample

Question: Name an important part of a coral reef and explain why it is important.

Grade level answer: Plants are an important part of a coral reef system. Plants are important because they provide a home, a place to hide and food for fish. In the text it says, "Coral reefs have many places where fish can live and hide". Plants are an important part of a coral reef.

Grade 6 Student Sample

Question: Name an important part of a coral reef and explain why it is important.

Grade level answer: Plants are an important part of a coral reef system. Plants are important because they provide a home for small fish, a place to hide from predators and food for herbivores. In the text it says, "Coral reefs have many places where fish can live and hide". Plants are an important part of a coral reef.

JUNIOR PARAGRAPH FORMAT

Topic (restate the question without the "W" word)	
Explanation (give an answer and explain why, using the word "because")	because _____ _____ _____
Example (a direct quote from the reading selection)	In the _____ it says, " _____ "
Conclusion (restate the Topic sentence)	

Now go back and check…

_____ Does my topic restate the question without the question word?

_____ Does my explanation answer the question "why?" by using the word "because"?

_____ Is my example a quote directly from the reading selection?

_____ Do I conclude by restating the topic sentence?

Grade Seven

By grade seven students should have a clear understanding of how a paragraph helps them to organize their thoughts. In grade seven students should be focused on using personal experiences to help them understand what they are reading. In that light, we include personal connections, with specific examples of the events within the TEEC paragraph. The paragraph actually becomes: Topic, Example, Explanation, Connection, Event, Conclusion. We continue to refer to it as TEEC since TEEC is a system that they have been learning about for several years and sticks in their minds.

A peer-editing checklist is listed at the bottom of the template to help students check their work.

Student Sample

Question: Will Anne be sent to live with Mrs. Blewett or be allowed to stay with Marilla and Matthew (in the book *Anne of Green Gables* by L.M. Montgomery)?

Grade level answer: Anne will get to stay with Matthew and Marilla. She will be allowed to stay because Marilla does not like Mrs. Blewett and has begun to take pity on Anne. In the novel it says, "I wouldn't give a dog I liked to that Blewett woman". This reminds me of the time my mom put our dog up for adoption. My family was very careful about finding a good owner. Anne will get to stay with Matthew and Marilla.

GRADE 7 PARAGRAPH FORMAT

Topic (restate the question without the "W" word)	
Explanation (give an answer and explain why, using the word "because")	**because** _____ _____ _____
Example (a direct quote from the reading selection)	In the _____ it says, " _____ "
My Connection (how does this relate to something you know?)	This reminds me of _____ _____
My Example (a specific example relating to your connection)	
Conclusion (restate the Topic sentence)	

Now go back and check…

_____ Does my topic restate the question without the question word?

_____ Does my explanation answer the question "why?" by using the word "because"?

_____ Is my example a quote directly from the reading selection?

_____ Do I have a connection related to my life?

_____ Do I tell what happened regarding the connection, with a specific example from my life?

_____ Do I conclude by restating the topic sentence?

Grade Eight

Finally, by grade eight students should be writing in TEEC style without even thinking about it. The emphasis becomes very focused on how the reading strategies – especially connections – help the students to understand what they are reading. The grade eight students go from simply using the strategies to being able to write about specifically how the strategies help their comprehension. Another sentence is added to the TEEC paragraph stating "How It Helps". That is, how the connection or other strategy helps the students' understanding of what they have read. The full paragraph used for answering reading comprehension questions becomes Topic, Explanation, Example, Connection, Event, How It Helps, Conclusion.

A checklist is included with the rubric to help students with self – editing. The extension for grade eight students is to be able to keep the TEEC style while sharing their own voice. By using their own voice, it takes away the mechanical paragraph format to make their own writing more interesting.

Student Sample

Question: Will Anne be sent to live with Mrs. Blewett or be allowed to stay with Marilla and Matthew (in the book *Anne of Green Gables* by L.M. Montgomery)?

Grade level answer: Anne will get to stay with Matthew and Marilla. She will be allowed to stay because Marilla does not like Mrs. Blewett and has begun to take pity on Anne. In the novel it says, "I wouldn't give a dog I liked to that Blewett woman". This reminds me of the time my mom put our dog up for adoption. My family was very careful about finding a good owner. This helps me to understand the text because I have a good idea of how Marilla was feeling when making the decision about what to do with Anne. Anne will get to stay with Matthew and Marilla.

Student voice answer: Marilla and Matthew will end up keeping Anne and Anne will love Green Gables. I predict this because Anne never really had a childhood, moving place to place and Marilla felt really bad for her. I also think that Marilla is going to keep Anne because she can connect with her because she understands what it is like not being loved by someone. As well, Matthew really wants to keep her. Matthew has hired Jerry Buote to help on the farm so Anne's being a girl is not really a concern. In the text it says "What if she, Marilla, should indulge Matthew's unaccountable whim and let her stay? He was set on it, and the child seemed a nice, teachable little thing". This reminds me of a book I read where Sam wanted a dog but his parents thought he was too irresponsible and couldn't look after the pet. They finally gave in and Sam got the dog, just like I think Marilla will give in and keep Anne. This connection helps me understand the situation in the text because I have read about similar decisions being made in past texts. These are my predictions for Anne.

GRADE 8 PARAGRAPH FORMAT

Topic (restate the question without the "W" word)	
Explanation (give an answer and explain why, using the word "because")	**because** _____ _____ _____
Example (a direct quote from the reading selection)	In the _____ it says, " _____ "
My Connection (how does this relate to something you know?)	This reminds me of _____ _____
My Example (a specific example relating to your connection)	
How It Helps Me Understand My Reading	
Conclusion (restate the Topic sentence)	

Now go back and check…

_____ Does my topic restate the question without the question word?

_____ Does my explanation answer the question "why?" by using the word "because"?

_____ Is my example a quote directly from the reading selection?

_____ Do I have a connection related to my life?

_____ Do I tell what happened regarding the connection, with a specific example from my life?

_____ Do I explain how my connection helps me to understand what I am reading?

_____ Do I conclude by restating the topic sentence?

23

TEEC and Tech

The TEEC system easily allows the integration of technology. In fact, there are a few technologies that actually help the TEEC system become more accessible to students who have difficulties with memory and processing. Technology can also be used to clarify aspects of TEEC with a large or a small group.

Using the TEEC templates and typing samples together while projecting onto a Smart Board® or a whiteboard is a very simple way to incorporate technology into teaching with The TEEC system. Later in this book you will find sample templates that can be used together as a class to share writing experiences within the TEEC system.

Technology such as Kurzweil 3000™ or a talking word processor can be a big help to students with memory or processing difficulties. These programs allow the user to scan texts into the computer or save texts into the program. The texts can then be read aloud to the user. This option makes the texts more accessible to all students. It is also a benefit to some students to hear the texts being read so that they may hear the flow of the text.

Once the text has been read, students may use highlighters within the program to highlight aspects of the text that they think will be important. By teaching students to use different colours for ideas that could help the different sentences of the TEEC paragraph, students will learn to identify significant ideas and not waste time with unneeded details. Those same colours can be used to highlight each sentence as the student answers a question that has been posed. This allows the students to visually understand the aspects needed in each answer and in each TEEC paragraph. The students can also see how the important aspects of the story relate to the questions they are answering. The anchor charts hanging in the classroom should also be colour coordinated to match the technology that students use.

For example, in my classroom the students chose to use blue highlighters for the Topic sentence, green for the Explanation, yellow for the Example and pink for the Conclusion.

The highlights mark each sentence like this:

The main idea of Beauty and the Beast is to love people for who they are on the inside. (blue highlight) This is the main idea because the story revolves around a monster who turns out to be really nice. (green highlight) In the text it says, "Then it started to say a few kind words, till in the end Beauty was amazed to discover that she was actually enjoying the conversation. The days passed and Beauty and the Beast became good friends". (yellow highlight) The main idea of the story is to love people for who they are on the inside. (purple highlight)

When new sentences are introduced, such as the Connection, Event or How It helps, new colours can be introduced. The highlighting idea transfers well from the technology into written work. Students can easily use standard highlighters while writing in order to keep their thoughts organized in an appropriate manner. For a time, the classroom teacher should expect and require the highlighting to happen on all activities. Gradually, students can be released back to writing without highlighters once the teacher is satisfied that the student understands what the TEEC paragraph should look like.

Be aware, you may find some students really enjoy adding colour to their work and may continue using highlighters even after they have been released back to regular written work.

Marking TEEC Paragraphs

What you look for when you are marking an activity or assignment really depends on the learning goals for that activity. In that respect there is no one correct way to evaluate a TEEC paragraph. However, when students are first learning the format it is important to be consistent in requiring that all reading responses must follow the TEEC format being taught. Many students will take short cuts and try to prove that they can give you an answer in a quicker fashion. To be successful, consistency is important. For the first little while it works well to evaluate based on the paragraph format, rather than the content. Most often the format forces the information in the answers to be reasonable anyway but marking the format will make students realize that it is important.

(Just a little secret…it makes marking very quick and easy too)

Here is a simple way to help students understand the importance of the TEEC format.
If there is a Topic sentence the paragraph receives a D.
If there is an Explanation using the word "because" the paragraph receives a C.
If there is an Example that is a quote directly from the text with quotation marks, the paragraph receives a B.
If there is a Conclusion sentence the paragraph receives a B+.

Marks of A or higher are only given to those students that are able to extend the paragraph beyond their grade level expectation. This means that once students are in grade eight they will also need to show a Connection, Connection Example, and How It Helps Me Understand, sentence in order to receive a B grade.

Grades that include a plus or minus such as C+ or C- should be given based on the content after the format is considered first.

The marking system used above assumes that a B level is considered to be at grade level.

On the following page you will find a rubric that may help clarify what to look for.

TEEC Paragraph Rubric

Category	Level 1	Level 2	Level 3	Level 4
Knowledge and Understanding	- includes 3 or less of the following: a topic sentence, three supporting details and a concluding sentence - uses only a few descriptive words	- includes 4 of the following: a topic sentence, three supporting details and a concluding sentence - uses some descriptive words	- includes topic sentence, three supporting details and a concluding sentence - uses a considerable number of descriptive words	- includes topic sentence, three or more interesting supporting details and a concluding sentence - uses many effective descriptive words
Thinking	- develops rough notes and revises notes with limited effectiveness	- develops rough notes and revises notes with some effectiveness	- develops rough notes and revises notes with considerable effectiveness	- develops rough notes and revises notes with a high degree of effectiveness
Communication	- uses a limited vocabulary (descriptive words) - there is limited evidence of the writer's voice (feelings, opinions, attitudes) - paragraph is unclear and/or does not flow - many major errors in spelling, grammar and punctuation	- uses some variety of vocabulary to add descriptive detail - there is some evidence of the writer's voice (feelings, opinions, attitudes) - paragraph is somewhat clear and/or has some evidence of flow - 1-2 major errors or 3-4 minor errors in grammar, spelling, and punctuation	- uses a wide variety of vocabulary to add effective description - there is clear evidence of the writer's voice (feelings, opinions, attitudes) - paragraph is clear and flows well - 1-2 minor errors in grammar, spelling and punctuation	- uses an extensive vocabulary that creates mental images for the reader - the writer's voice is clear and sustains the reader's interest - paragraph is clear and flows effectively from beginning to end - no errors in spelling, grammar, and punctuation
Application	- uses the paragraph outline with limited effectiveness - uses a variety of sentence types and structures with limited effectiveness	- uses the paragraph outline with some effectiveness - uses a variety of sentence types and structures with some effectiveness	- uses the paragraph outline with considerable effectiveness - uses a variety of sentence types and structures with considerable effectiveness	- uses the paragraph outline with a high degree of effectiveness - uses a variety of sentence types and structures to sustain readers' interest

Accountable Talk with TEEC

The TEEC system provides easy opportunities for students to be involved in accountable talk in the classroom. Whether it be as part of the writing process or reading comprehension, the simplicity of the TEEC format allows students to talk about it easily. Breaking apart sentences and examining the relevance of information is an easy way to promote talk and make sure that students understand what they need to include within their answers and their writing.

The TEEC paragraph format is also easy for students to self-evaluate and peer-assess. When they are given a rubric or checklist that follows the format requirements above, students will be able to help each other determine whether or not their answer is completed correctly.

Using the TEEC system and a little practice, students will be able to help each other create clear, fluent paragraphs.

How Will You Know it's Working?

The big question for any educational endeavor is: How will you know it's working?

On many occasions over the past few years I have been introduced to new ideas. Whether in Literacy or Math or Physical Education, it doesn't really matter what area of education you are in, new ideas are being brought forth on a regular basis. Each time a new idea is promoted there are always teachers who want to try it and others who would rather stick to what they already know. Usually the reason is because they already have ideas that work for them and are reluctant to do something new without knowing that it will work in their classroom. When TEEC was first introduced to the staff at my school, it was a very tough sell. Many people claimed that it worked in my classroom because my students were already smarter than their students. Others chose to keep their own style because the end result that they had in their mind was the same as what TEEC would provide. It took about four years to finally get those last few teachers onboard with the school-wide program. They eventually realized that the students found the TEEC system easier to follow than other ideas that had been used in the past.

Of course, we all need to be able to see results in our classroom to truly believe in any new practice. There are a few simple ways to see that TEEC is providing results. Here is a list of things to look for:

1. All answers written in paragraph form.
2. Paragraphs have four sentences.
3. Paragraphs start with a topic sentence.
4. Paragraphs have a second sentence including the word "because".
5. Paragraphs have an example, quoted directly from the text.
6. Paragraphs have a concluding sentence that resembles the topic sentence.
7. Students stop complaining about how much work it is to write a paragraph and begin using paragraphs without being told to do so.
8. Students begin to use the TEEC structure across all subjects.
9. Students can easily read and explain their answer orally.
10. Students work is easy for the teacher to read because it flows in an organized fashion.

Students Carry TEEC On

In putting this book together it got me thinking about former students that I had in my classes who learned TEEC beginning in grade six. I can recall at least one student every year who took the time to return from high school to tell me that they are still using the TEEC paragraph and it has helped them to do well in English class. They seem amazed that I was telling the truth when I told them that they would be able to use this structure through high school and into university.

With one particular group of students I had the benefit of teaching them in grade six, seven and eight. I asked two of those students to come back and talk to me about their TEEC experience and how they remember it. Matthew began using TEEC with me in grade six.

He moved into a different grade seven classroom and then returned to my class in grade eight, where TEEC really took hold for him. Devyani was first in my class in grade seven and was a culprit for loading the page with as much information as possible. She was in my class again in grade eight and was challenged to write in a much more concise form.

As Devyani and Matthew recalled they came out of grade five using the APE strategy. They were unhappy and unsure about learning a new structure. Devyani recalled not really "getting it" when TEEC was presented. She did not understand why she should change what she already knew. Matthew suggested that his peers felt the same way. They did not want to change what they had learned in grade five. The TEEC paragraph appeared to be more work and the students did not like it. Understanding how to get all of their information into four sentences was a struggle but once the sentences were broken down and then reconstructed, TEEC clicked.

Both Matthew and Devyani, in discussion, agreed that TEEC turned out to be a better and easier paragraph with which to work. They stated that the TEEC system helped them to explain ideas in a better fashion; it was easy to follow so that the resulting paragraph turned out right every time, and it looked nicer. They also found that the basic TEEC format was easy to expand upon, using extra explanation and examples.

Devyani felt that constant use and the fact that their evaluation was based on the TEEC structure, forced students to transition to TEEC. By the time the students were through grade eight they wrote naturally using the TEEC system and realized that their writing flowed well. The TEEC system was not a challenge; it was just "how things were done".

The TEEC system forced students to explain their answers and students began to realize that explanation was important. As Matthew said in our discussions, "With APE, students didn't feel they needed to really understand what they were writing". With TEEC, it forced students to link their explanation to the answer and they showed understanding by having a relevant example. Devyani's statement summed TEEC up very well. "TEEC taught us that it was more about quality than quantity," she said.

Now in high school, Devyani and Matthew use TEEC as the basis of all of their writing. Several other students have confirmed the same thing – TEEC works. These students have taken the TEEC system and expanded it on their own terms to fit their high school needs. Sometimes that means more than one explanation per paragraph or simply adding one's own voice by using different wording. Matthew made it clear, "The first E is key. The Explanation. That pulls the whole answer together." The students agree that it is TEEC that they are using. It is a habit that has led to success.

What's Next?

You've used the paragraph structure. The students are answering questions with proof. Now what? Throughout these pages TEEC has been talked about as a system. What's next is that it's time to move from a paragraph structure to a literacy system.

The original paragraph structure that you have been reading about covers the reading part of literacy with the help of strong teaching. The TEEC paragraph has also helped students with oral language since it forces them to speak with fluency and provide proof for what they are saying. It also forces them to listen to the opinions and proofs of other students. The final piece of the TEEC literacy system is to incorporate TEEC into student writing. As Matthew and Devyani have made evident in the previous section, writing with TEEC leads to success.

Writing with TEEC

The TEEC system transfers to the writing process to make non-fiction writing easy for students to understand. As mentioned in earlier sections, TEEC encourages explanation of a topic with proof that the explanation is correct. Good non-fiction writing requires the same traits.
The TEEC system is beneficial for:
- Expository writing
    - Any type of report, such as Informational reports, Analytical reports, Historical reports, Newspaper reports, Scientific reports
- Persuasive writing
    - Any writing where making an argument is important will be enhanced by the topic, explanation, example, conclusion style of the TEEC system

The sections that follow provide templates and examples to show how TEEC helps students write more clearly. Flow and proof are evident in their writing because the paragraph format forces students to be more specific in their explanations and examples. For instance, when we ask students to write an essay to prove that Walt Disney was a great man, the TEEC format forces them to explain why they believe he was great and prove it with a researched quote. The Example becomes an easily visible deciding factor for whether or not the students have proven their point.

While transitioning the TEEC paragraph into more significant forms of writing remember to focus on format first. The TEEC style provides a simple format so that students know what information is important for their writing. Once students understand the type of information is needed in a report – or whatever type of writing is chosen – then it will become necessary to review word choice and conventions. The nice thing is that sentence structure and fluency are built into the TEEC system.

One complaint that I have heard about TEEC is that it's too plain and can be a little bit boring to read. I don't disagree. At times it can be boring to read but it is nice to be able to clearly understand what I am reading while I am assessing student work. The more creative part of non-fiction writing – the voice – is the extension piece when teaching writing. Once students understand the format of the written piece they are working on and have been able to use clear and interesting words, then it will be time to teach them about using their own voice in their writing. The use of one's own voice truly happens when students understand how to write and what it means to have fluency within their writing. The basic TEEC structure should still be evident, simply with added sentences or rearranged wordings to make the message more appealing to a given audience.

Beginning where things are simple is the best way to ensure future success.

Writing Templates

The templates that follow can help students organize their writing. Each template shows how the TEEC format is used within each style of writing. There is a basic Expository template for introducing students to that form of writing, including persuasive essays. There is also an Informational Report template for students who are trying to put a larger piece of writing together using the TEEC format.

Expository Writing:
Ideas and Drafting

Name: _____

Due Date: _____

Component:	Due Date:

Organizing your expository writing:

Introduction • Briefly answer the 5 W's • Thesis - state your position in a clear, concise, sentence • A thesis is not "I think, I believe, or In my opinion", it must be a solid statement	☐ Who ☐ What ☐ When ☐ Where ☐ Why ☐ How ☐ Thesis statement
Body • Paragraph #1 • Topic, Explanation, Example, Conclusion	☐ Support idea #1 ☐ Relate personal detail, experience, reasoning, or fact to support your position
Body • Paragraph #2 • Topic, Explanation, Example, Conclusion	☐ Support idea #2 ☐ Relate personal detail, experience, reasoning, or fact to support your position
Body • Paragraph #3 • Topic, Explanation, Example, Conclusion	☐ Support idea #2 ☐ Relate personal detail, experience, reasoning, or fact to support your position
Conclusion • Restate your ideas and thesis	☐ Reflect on your experience and explain the "Big Picture" or the "Big Idea" behind your reasoning throughout this piece of writing

The question/issue I feel most prepared to write about is _____

_____

I want to write about this because _____

_____

_____

_____

Use the checklist to ensure your introduction is complete.

Introduction	
• Briefly answer the 5 W's • Thesis - state your position in a clear, concise, sentence • A thesis is not "I think, I believe, or In my opinion", it must be a solid statement	☐ Who ☐ What ☐ When ☐ Where ☐ Why ☐ How ☐ Thesis statement

Write a paragraph that includes the 5 Ws using descriptive language.

_____

_____

_____

_____

_____

_____

What position do you stand to defend? Be sure to make your statement clear.

_____

_____

_____

_____

My Thoughts Page

Let's get those ideas onto paper. Who, what, where, why, when, how?
Use words, descriptors and pictures.

Use the checklist to guide your thinking.

Body	
Body • Paragraph #1 • Topic, Explanation, Example, Conclusion	☐ Support idea #1 ☐ Relate personal detail, experience, reasoning, or fact to support your position

Topic: _____

_____

_____

Explanation:_____

_____

_____

_____

Example: _____

_____

_____

Conclusion: _____

_____

_____

_____

Use the checklist to guide your thinking.

Body	Support idea #2
• Paragraph #2 • Topic, Explanation, Example, Conclusion	☐ Support idea #2 ☐ Relate personal detail, experience, reasoning, or fact to support your position

Topic: _____

_____

_____

Explanation:_____

_____

_____

_____

Example: _____

_____

_____

Conclusion: _____

_____

_____

_____

Use the checklist to guide your thinking.

Body	
• Paragraph #3 • Topic, Explanation, Example, Conclusion	☐ Support idea #3 ☐ Relate personal detail, experience, reasoning, or fact to support your position

Topic: _____

_____

_____

Explanation:_____

_____

_____

_____

Example: _____

_____

_____

_____

Conclusion: _____

_____

_____

_____

Use the checklist to guide your conclusion.

Conclusion • Restate your ideas and thesis	☐ Reflect on your experience and explain the "Big Picture" or the "Big Idea" behind your reasoning throughout this piece of writing

☐ Restate your position
☐ Briefly restate your ideas
☐ Reflect on the "Big Idea"
☐ Finish it off

Conclusion: _____

_____

_____

_____

_____

_____

_____

_____

_____

Revise and Edit

Expository Revision Checklist

Does your introduction:
- ❑ establish a position
- ❑ introduce the main ideas
- ❑ include an answer to the question/issue

Does your body:
- ❑ have at least three paragraphs
- ❑ have TEEC paragraphs
- ❑ explain your position

Does your conclusion:
- ❑ restate your position
- ❑ restate your ideas
- ❑ reflect on the "Big Idea"
- ❑ wrap it all together

Does your essay:
- ❑ include at least 5 adjectives - Underline them!
- ❑ create good feelings about your position
- ❑ include strong reasons for your position
- ❑ use a variety of vocabulary and sentences
- ❑ state only one position

Have you:
- ❑ changed at least 5 adjectives or adverbs to make them more descriptive
- ❑ read your essay aloud and improved upon the fluency of your essay
- ❑ crossed out and rewritten at least one sentence in each paragraph
- ❑ stayed on one topic

Now...
Polish your essay. Make it look and sound great.
Typing it is a great option.

Informational Report Writing:

Name: _____

Due Date: _____

Component:	Due Date:

Organizing your informational report writing:

Title Page   • Title   • By   • For   • Due
Table of Contents   • A list of all main sections with page numbers
Synopsis   • A brief summary of what is in the report
Introduction   • What are you writing and why?
Section 1   • What information do you have?
Section 2   • What information do you have?
Section 3   • What information do you have?
Conclusion   • Wrap it together
Synopsis   • Summarize your report
Bibliography/Resources   • A properly formatted list of resources

The topic I feel most prepared to explore is _____

_____

I want to explore this because _____

_____

_____

_____

43

Use the checklist to ensure your introduction is complete.

Introduction	
• Open your report • Briefly answer the 5 W's with reference to your career path • What do you hope to learn • State your ultimate goal	☐ Who ☐ What ☐ When ☐ Where ☐ Why ☐ How

Write a paragraph that details the 5 Ws of your report.

_____

_____

_____

_____

_____

_____

_____

_____

_____

_____

My Thoughts Page

Let's get those ideas onto paper. Who, what, where, why, when, how?
Use words, descriptors and pictures.

Use the checklist to guide your thinking.

Section 1 <ul><li>State your information, explain why it is important, give an example of how you know it is important, conclude the paragraph</li><li>Topic, Explanation, Example, Conclusion</li></ul>	☐ Support idea #1 ☐ Relate personal detail, experience, reasoning, or fact to support your position ☐ You may want more than one paragraph

Topic: _____

_____

_____

Explanation:_____

_____

_____

_____

Example: _____

_____

_____

Conclusion: _____

_____

_____

Use the checklist to guide your thinking.

Section 2	
• State your information, explain why it is important, give an example of how you know it is important, conclude the paragraph • Topic, Explanation, Example, Conclusion	☐ Support idea #2 ☐ Relate personal detail, experience, reasoning, or fact to support your position ☐ You may want more than one paragraph

Topic: _____

_____

_____

Explanation:_____

_____

_____

_____

Example: _____

_____

_____

Conclusion: _____

_____

_____

Use the checklist to guide your thinking.

Section 3	☐ Support idea #3
• State your information, explain why it is important, give an example of how you know it is important, conclude the paragraph • Topic, Explanation, Example, Conclusion	☐ Relate personal detail, experience, reasoning, or fact to support your position ☐ You may want more than one paragraph

Topic: _____

_____

_____

Explanation:_____

_____

_____

_____

Example: _____

_____

_____

Conclusion: _____

_____

_____

Use the checklist to guide your conclusion.

Conclusion	☐ Reflect on your experience and explain the "Big Picture" or the "Big Idea" behind your reasoning throughout this piece of writing
• Restate your purpose and main findings	

☐ Restate your purpose
☐ Briefly restate your main findings
☐ Reflect on the "Big Idea"
☐ Finish it off

Conclusion: _____

_____

_____

_____

_____

_____

_____

_____

_____

Use the checklist to ensure your synopsis is complete.

Synopsis	
Synopsis • Summarize your report • Briefly answer the 5 W's with reference to your career path • State your ultimate goal	☐ Who ☐ What ☐ When ☐ Where ☐ Why ☐ How ☐ Career goal

Write a summary of your report. Although this goes first, it may be completed last.

_____

_____

_____

_____

_____

_____

_____

_____

_____

_____

A Successful Report

Your findings should be presented in a written report format.

The Report Checklist
- ❑ A catchy title
- ❑ A synopsis of the report
- ❑ Headings for each section
- ❑ Subheadings within the sections
- ❑ Full paragraphs
- ❑ Pictures with captions
- ❑ Charts or graphs
- ❑ Primary and secondary information (sidebars?)
- ❑ Glossary
- ❑ Bibliography/Resource list

Have you revised/edited your report:
- ❑ Changed at least 5 adjectives or adverbs to make them more descriptive
- ❑ Read your report aloud and improved upon the fluency of your essay
- ❑ Crossed out and rewritten at least one sentence in each paragraph
- ❑ Stayed on one topic

Due Dates:

Introduction: _____

Section 1: _____

Section 2: _____

Section 3: _____

Synopsis: _____

Final Report: _____

TEEC and Inquiry

Using TEEC to help drive inquiry projects is also all about making the transition into written work very simple.

A common approach to inquiry for most students is to Google and type in a keyword. They usually follow that by clicking on the first or second link they find and writing down a whole bunch of information on a blank sheet of paper. Once they have written all they can from one link, they'll click on the next one and write down more information on the same page. In the age of information, finding facts is not usually the difficult part of an assignment. The difficult part is to organize those facts into a clear written work.

Using templates from the TEEC system, student writing is organized even before they begin. Each template offers a spot to indicate where the information came from in order to facilitate a resource list. Each template also provides specific areas to indicate the question being answered or topic being discussed, an answer or discussion point, an explanation, proof, and a final point of interest. The T E E C coincides with each section so that students can then transfer their information into clear paragraphs.

The information from the inquiry can be made into paragraphs which can then be transferred to writing templates and finally into a polished format. That is the TEEC system.

Inquiry Templates

The inquiry template used by students in grades three to eight is on the next three pages.

Inquiry Process:
Ideas and Drafting

Name: _____

Due Date: _____

Organizing your inquiry:

Exploring • Choose a topic • Develop a "Big Idea" question • Develop secondary research questions	☐ What is the topic? ☐ What is the main question? ☐ What are some other questions?
Investigating • Design a plan • Find sources of information • Decide on a focus for the research	☐ What are you researching first? ☐ Other ideas to research ☐ Sources listed ☐ Stay on one question/idea
Processing • Analyse the information • Organize and synthesize the findings	☐ What will you keep? ☐ What can be discarded? ☐ What order should it be in?
Creating • Make and present a final product • Self and peer assessment	☐ How will the information be presented? ☐ Who has read your product?
TEEC • Organize your research into TEEC paragraphs	☐ Topic, Explanation, Example, Conclusion

The topic I feel most prepared to write about is _____

_____

I want to write about this topic because _____

_____

The Topic: _____   Name:_____

Big Idea Question:	Research Question:

Sources of Information:

Information Gathered:

Topic Sentence:

A 1st Possible Explanation:	A 1st Possible Example from the Text:
A 2nd Possible Explanation:	A 2nd Possible Example from the Text:
A 3rd Possible Explanation:	A 3rd Possible Example from the Text:
A 4th Possible Explanation:	A 4th Possible Example from the Text:

Concluding Sentence:

From Classroom Teacher to School-Wide Program

The fact that you have even picked up this book suggests that you are looking for something to help students succeed in literacy. We know that schools everywhere are trying to do the same. By bringing the TEEC system into your classroom your students are being prepared for future grades and ultimately jobs.

As you introduce the TEEC system to students many will complain that it is too much work. As you work throughout the year students will begin to use it for everything they write. One morning I asked students to write down a question that they would ask someone who runs the Air Canada Centre where the Toronto Maple Leafs play. I needed the questions so that when the person came to talk to the class he would have answers prepared for them. I expected that I would receive one sentence from each student in a question format. What I received was a class set of TEEC paragraphs explaining the question and why they would ask their specific question.

With this type of training and success students can easily take the TEEC paragraph into the next grade each year. However, if the next grade teacher is not requiring TEEC structures many students will get lazy and revert back to answers without full explanation or proof. Because of this, it is beneficial to everyone if the TEEC system becomes a school-wide initiative.

How to Make It Happen

In order to make the TEEC system a school-wide program many things have to be in place. You will need a school community that is supportive of each other, an administrator that is willing to try a new idea, a lead TEEC teacher and a small group of staff that are ready to stand behind the lead teacher in implementing the program.

The order in which you get this support is not necessarily significant. When I began my journey I didn't even know this was going to become as successful as it has become. Once I realized how well the TEEC system was working in my classroom I introduced the idea to my grade partners. Those people became my support group that would stand with me each time I introduced the TEEC idea to another group of my colleagues. We stood together and showed the school Principal that the system was effective. Once he was on board, we slowly introduced it throughout the school.

The slow introduction was important. We decided to introduce the TEEC system as something we would like to try in each grade. I say this is important because within each school there are staff members who are adverse to change. We wanted to ensure there wasn't any dissension in the staff and so allowed people to try TEEC if they were interested. At all times, my support group would talk to others about the success that the system has shown in their classrooms. As time progressed and more people were on board, the principal required that TEEC be used in each classroom. This process took time even with the push from the Principal. There were still teachers who did not want to change. The total changeover took about three years but once everyone was on board, the full value of the TEEC system could be realized.

Be prepared for a slow, sometimes difficult implementation. Find a strong support group first and then, most importantly, believe in what you are implementing.

Administrator Roles

The administrator's role is significant, yet minimal at the same time. The "to-do" part of the administrator's role is the minimal part. It is up to teachers to implement the system in the classroom. The significant part is that the administrator needs to be strong as part of the support group standing behind the lead teacher. It is important that the administrator be the one who encourages teachers in each grade to use TEEC. He or she must be willing to sell the system to the staff. The administrator must also be willing to support the system when questions arise from Superintendents or other Board officials. In order to provide this support, the administrator is going to have to have some clear proof that the system works. Be prepared to supply this support with information from classrooms throughout the school.

What About Special Education Requirements

The TEEC system has many benefits for students with special needs. Because the TEEC system relies strongly on specific formats and templates, it is very easy for students with special needs to follow. The program allows teachers to use scaffolding techniques to teach these students one step at a time. Even those students who need to work with computers and other technology are well served by the TEEC system since all the templates can be made available in assistive technology programs.

Staff Turnover

The second biggest struggle to the school-wide program, after the initial buy-in period, is dealing with staff turnover. This is a difficult item to deal with because teachers come and go every year and because new teachers bring new ideas. While we don't want to squash new ideas, we do want to make sure that the students are receiving a consistent message from grade-to-grade. The great thing is that as long as the basic TEEC format and message is being taught, new ideas can enhance the program.

In order to make sure that all staff know the TEEC system it is important to take time at the beginning of each school year – ideally at a staff meeting before the first day – to present the system and explain how it is used within the school. Hopefully the principal has already talked about the TEEC system when interviewing new staff so that they are prepared to adjust before the year starts. The other thing that is necessary is to have a full package of TEEC expectations, templates and examples available for each new staff member so that they are not left trying to figure it out on their own. Their own copy of this book might be the perfect resource to get new staff members up to speed quickly.

Top of the Class

The TEEC system makes reading and writing easy for students. Once they understand the format, grade level achievement is not far behind. Over the years the TEEC system has consistently benefited those students who were struggling to bump up to the next level. With the simple and clear format of the TEEC system these student have been able to find and to communicate the information they needed to be successful. The TEEC system has also pushed those students who were already at grade level to go further and extend their understanding of reading and writing. When a grade three student masters the grade three template, allow that student to move on to the grade four template. As long as the writing remains clear, concise and in the correct format, that student's communication will improve. The simplicity of the TEEC system has allowed some younger students communicate well beyond their grade level.

Like any beneficial activity, TEEC takes an effort on the part of the Teacher. The teacher must be consistent and must commit to the clear expectations of the TEEC system. With effort, the rewards will come. TEEC can help your students achieve today and in the future, at the top of their class.

APPENDIX

Another TEEC Template

Topic Sentence (tells the main idea of your entire paragraph – use the question or prompt to help)	
Explanation (explains what you mean and gives more specific details so the reader understand exactly what you are trying to explain)	
Example (includes examples to prove what you are saying – is specific)	
Explanation (gives more details about your topic answering the question)	
Example (includes an example to prove your last explanation – is specific)	
Conclusion (restates the topic sentence in slightly different words)	

Topic

Explanation

Example

Conclusion

Resources

"Beauty and the Beast." Original Tale:, N.p., n.d. Web. 17 Apr. 2013
http://www.fpx.de/fp/Disney/Tales/BeautyAndTheBeast.html.

Connolly, Matthew, and Devyani Premkumar. "Former Students Using TEEC." Personal interview. 26 Mar. 2013

"The Doorway to Information." DDSB Library. N.p., n.d. Web. 10 Apr. 2013.
http://library.ddsbschools.ca/

Montgomery, L. M., and Caroline Parry. *The Anne of Green Gables Novels*. New York: Bantam, 1998. Print.

"6+1 Traits® Definitions Education Northwest." 6 1 Trail® Definitions Education Northwest. N.p., n.d. Web 7 Apr. 2013. <http://educationnorthwest.org/resource/503>

54162101R00039

Made in the USA
Charleston, SC
27 March 2016